Table of Contents

Foreword

I never considered myself a writer. I grew up in Silicon Valley, home of the "rat" race, where everyone is just trying to live the American Dream and make a ton of money. As a kid, I was a bit of a shy nerd and never popular but excelled in school. As I grew older, I started to get attention from guys and felt the pressure to be beautiful, perfect, and well-liked. I felt like I lost my identity because I was so concerned about what everyone else thought instead of if I liked myself or not. I constantly tried to plan everything in life as if I was in total control. I worried if I would find the right guy, job, home, etc. instead of wondering if I was happy or content with who I was and where I was going.

One day, feeling overwhelmed and emotionally drained by something not going my way, I wrote down a few words which became my first poem. I found myself feeling that there must be more to life than material success and the comfort factor of being in a relationship. I started to look for ways to "slow down" and enjoy life without letting go of responsibilities. Through daily meditation and becoming "mindful" (enjoying and savoring the present moment), I felt compelled to continue to write. This surprised me, as I never liked writing, but enjoyed the predictability and stability of math.

I wrote "Butterfly" as a way to document questions/struggles/emotions I was having while striving to learn and grow in our ever-changing society. Despite whatever background you come from, I hope that reading it will encourage you to look at your own personal journey through life and evaluate your happiness and current dreams.

Though I desired to have one and tried, I have never given birth to a child. "Butterfly" is my way of giving birth to something that I hope will make a difference. I would have named my daughter, Isabella Evangeline, thus the pseudonym.

I want to thank you for reading my journey (ahead of time) and hope you enjoy it!

Much love,

Isabella Evangeline

To everyone questioning the root of their happiness

Desiring Wisdom

Craving Peace

Striving to become a better version

of themselves

Today

Each day
is new
is a chance
to change
to love
to learn
to grow.
sit for awhile...
and feel the sun
hear the joy
in the air
Breathe in...happiness
Breathe out...disappointment
Cherish your friends
Love your family
Forgive yourself
Forgive others
Be kind
Be real
Dream big
Work hard
But play harder.
Enjoy this moment
Right now.

Truth

i desire
to see
things as they truly are
and not what
i dreamt them to be
or my distorted
Perception
of what is.
is it possible
to be happy in Truth
and see the beauty
in every living thing
i do not want
to be content
in delusion
because I cannot
Accept the Truth.
isn't it beautiful
to look at the blueness of the sky
to hear the birds sing
and see the trees
sway in the wind.
to know I am free
to be my unique self
is the truest
Truth.

the question

do I need
to ask
the right question
to get the Truth?
or does the Truth
come out
even if no inquiry
is made?
do we even need to speak
for answers?
or can we stay silent
and quietly observe
and conclude
without critique?
can we accept the Truth
as it stands in front of us?
or do we shove it aside
because we don't like it?
must Truth cause pain?
or will it free us from the burden
of not knowing....

the fall

i thought i had everything...
a brand-new home
nice things
a steady job
just married
to a man i wanted
for so long
my whole future
was in front of me.
a fairytale to some.
But then why...
the fierce arguments
unwavering unhappiness
the endless tears
the disrespect
the jealousy
on both sides
How can you love someone
who turns on you
and treats you...
like a stranger.
How can you lay down
next to someone
who feels 100 miles away?
Deep i fell
into an abyss
into emptiness
and despair.
But slowly
I climbed
I fought my way out
and found
the person
I really was meant to be.

a version of Me

As i was walking
i came upon a woman
who looked exactly
like me
But she was glowing...
Effervescent
radiating happiness
and joy.
First thought... Confusion.
Second thought... Envy.
Third thought... Anger.
Fourth thought... Amazement.
What's your secret?
i asked.
I love and accept myself
was her answer.

Beauty

It exists in everything
every human being
If i look hard enough
i see true beauty
Everytime...
i see someone smile
or laugh
or share
or be kind.
The surface is an illusion
a deception
not a true reflection
of one's character
or heart.
Don't be fooled
if your confidence
is in youth
or the idea of perfection
You will be left
Thirsty
always wanting more...
If you value
Love
Kindness
Honesty
Knowledge
You will
Be fulfilled
and the constant
obsession of beauty
on the surface level
will fade away
and free you

to become
More.

imperfections

why do we all
Strive to be perfect
when perfect is boring.
there's nothing
to look beyond
with perfection.
Nothing to determine
Nothing to dream about
when it's placed in front of you.

Two choices
A perfect diamond
to show off to others.
or one with imperfections
for others to discover
To analyze
To speculate
To Relate to.

body

i have been given this body
to reside in
my entire life
Who I am
is trapped inside
waiting to be found.
You see only my body
my expressions
but do you know
who i am?
my struggles
my thoughts
my beliefs
my true feelings
are invisible
Unless i decide
to show you.
I am Me
not my body.

seen

i long to be Seen
for who i am
the question is...
am I showing others
the real Me?
i need to be vulnerable
Truthful
so you will see ME
what a joy
it must be
to have someone
who is not Blinded by
their perception of
who I am
but knows who is inside me
i must fight the desire
to be liked.
And show others
the true person
that lies beneath.

the shell

You look at me
but you do not See me
i do not smile
because i am naïve
but because i accept myself
for my flaws.
i do not laugh
because i'm stupid
but because you need
to have a sense of humor
to offset heartache and pain.
i have my own opinion
not because i want to fight you
but because i'm passionate
about what i believe.
i'm quiet
not because i'm complacent
but because i desire to become
a better listener
and take the time to understand
my surroundings.
i speak up
Not to make you feel
Inadequate
but because i care about you
and want to help.
i wish you could
Discover what lies
Deep inside
of me.

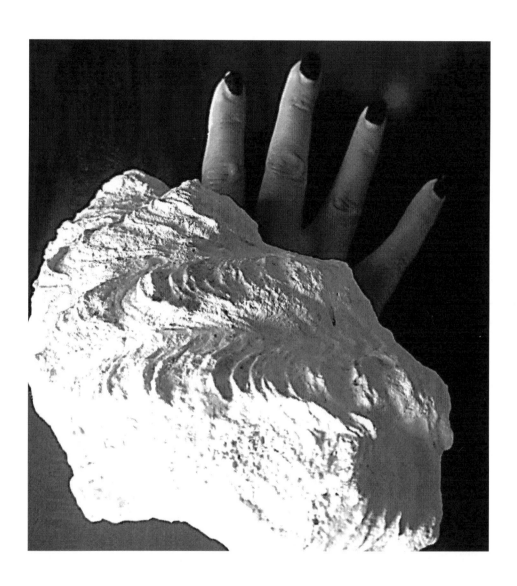

the cycle

i was young
i was foolish
i doubted
that i was enough
i felt so flawed
i wanted so badly
to be loved
that I was willing
to find it
in anyone
who could give me
That feeling
That look
I desired.
i didn't know
what love was
Not a feeling
but a commitment
Not showering me
with gifts
but respect
Not worshipping my appearance
and expecting perfection
but accepting my whole self
and surrounding me
Protecting me with love
and devotion.
I'm stepping off...
and stepping onto
Uncharted ground.

the past

He was everything
Yet he gave me
Nothing.
I was stripped bare...
Wandering in a desert
Searching for water
For sustenance.
I was left to decide
My path
My direction
Emaciated
I made a choice
And I regret
Nothing.

the Split

It feels like Agony
half my body has been
Ripped away.
as I bleed out
so do my emotions
and I am left
to patch myself up.
i know I will heal...
eventually
but how do I cope
with the pain...
NOW?

Isolation
because no one knows
what to say or do.
being alone
i feel comfortable
because no eyes are on me.
Solitude
makes me strong
all that Love goes
to me
and no one else.

Now I am Whole
not because of another
but because I have stuffed myself
With Self-love.

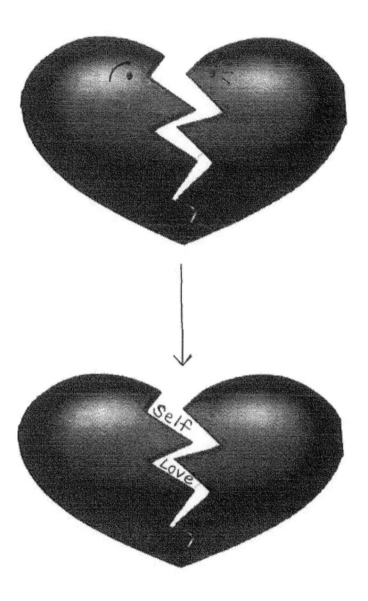

waves

i was sailing
in the water
so calm
peaceful
Expected
along came
beautiful destruction
taking me on
another path
not intended
scared
i resisted
i struggled
but the destination
was beyond
my wildest dreams.

the dive

it started with a conversation
i decided to dive deeper
into the depths
of your heart.
i didn't want a surface answer
but one that required
vulnerability
and Trust.
i wondered
what would I find?
something valuable
i would treasure
or a wreck
so uncanny
hidden
not ready to be discovered.
Will you dive in
after me
as I fall so deep
into waters
so dark
Unexplored
where no one
has been before.

the One

is there only One
out there for me?
Waiting...
for our paths
to cross
or is it
a decision I make
when I meet that person
that makes me feel like...
Home.
finally deciding to commit
and grab
onto that person
and never let them go
like a floating leaf
on a stream
that you will never
see again unless
You pick it up.

the onion

Have the courage
to peel me
layer by layer
to find me
my authentic self.
The outside world
Cannot see me
Cannot know me
just by looking hard.
As you peel
will i make you cry
or will I cry when
I see the effort
you have put in
To understand
To love
To get to know
Me.

eyes

if I look
into your eyes
will I see you...
in there?
your soul
your heart
the real you.
I want to go
Deeper with you
until I see your
Desire
Passion
vulnerability
Fighting to
connect with me.
just you and me
Exists
and everyone else...
fades away.

honesty

it's everything
to me
Love
is nothing
without
Honesty.
Patience
i must have
to see
what's revealed
in front of me
But I'm afraid...
to fall in love
because
it's already happening
with you.

transparency

I look at You
and see me
which gives me comfort
to be myself.
when you are not around
i long for you
no one else
can quench my thirst
My hunger
for your company.
to share a few words
feeds my soul
makes me smile
for the rest of the day.
I get nervous
sometimes
because I feel
Naked
in your eyes
you seem to see
right through me
Understand me
like we are meant to be.

the force

Love happens
when it's ready
It can't be coerced
or demanded
or forced
it arrives at your doorstep
when it wants to
Uninvited
an unexpected guest
you didn't know would come.
don't search for it
you won't find it
if you're looking
it will hide from you.
i'm not ready
for that feeling
that will turn me
inside out
or reeling
onto the floor.

temptation

what If
i never met you
would i be me
Today
or someone else
laying back
Dreaming of
someone like you.
do you even know
how much i admire
your tenacity
Respect
your convictions
Value
your advice
treasure
our friendship.
it's a mystery
how our paths crossed
minds touched
hearts melted
bodies ached
lines crossed
and we'll
never be the same
again.

the wilderness

His passion for learning unraveled me
His intellect seduced me
His sharp wit met me halfway
the softness of his skin stole my breath and I froze
His vulnerability brought me to tears…

His gentleness is to be desired
His scent cradles me and holds me tight
His mind caressed mine and would not leave my thoughts
but I know nothing of his Heart.

part two

I respect his wisdom as he is not quick to speak
His imperfections entice me
He has many layers which I have not discovered
will I have the opportunity to "see" more…
i don't know…
His weaknesses show me that he is human
and my weakness for him reminds me I am human
as I had no idea that I would feel, like…THIS.

is THIS a feeling I should act on
or is it meant to wander around in my soul
like a lost hiker trying to find the way home?
i still do not know what THIS is
but that's ok…because it has awakened me
and now i belong to the Wilderness…and i am Home.

the seed

you planted a seed
in my heart
it keeps growing
Wildly
Uncontrollably
in all directions
you water it
with your kindness
Love
Sincerity
Honesty
Loyalty
the fruit
is sweet
delicious
the best thing
i've ever tasted.
i pray that
it will never
stop producing
what makes me
feel alive.

the art of not knowing

do we ever know
how deeply one feels
for us
Loves us
unless we are told?
we cannot feel the depth
the magnitude
the secret longing
of another's emotion
unless its revealed or seen.
how many people have loved us
and we have been ignorant
Distracted by another
who hasn't the slightest
interest?
Take notice
of your surroundings
and treasure the people
that show you kindness
Love
and Respect.

the assumption

They left
at the same time.
it made me
want to cry.
my Imagination
took over
my rational mind.
i started to sweat
i raged inside.
i felt betrayed.
my unknown feelings
were rapidly bleeding out
and i was helpless...
there was
nothing
i could do or say
to make myself
feel better
or calm down.
Now i must wait
patiently
for the Truth.

the mind

it can trick you
it races
it wants to control...
Everything.
Hungry for knowledge
Starving for facts.
it wants...
precise decisions
exact answers.
it's smart
and cunning
desperate to change
your opinion.
it never gets tired
it can be your ally
or your worst enemy.
its message is important
but trust
and listen to your heart.

the green-eyed Monster

its imaginary
and a lie
it eats and devours
every good part of us
to make us feel inadequate
for no reason.

Envy is a waste of time.
The opposite of Truth.
Contaminating us
it steals our light
and throws us into Darkness.
You are unique
and perfectly You.
everything you have been given
is a gift
is for A reason.
You are beautiful
in your own way.
Don't ever entertain the thought
of not being You
and wanting to be...
someone else.

two sides

i love him
He doesn't love me.
He's always in my thoughts
i'm never in his.
i look into his eyes
He doesn't see me.
i'm going to push myself away.

She's the love of my life
i mean nothing to her.
i can't get her out of my mind.
She barely looks at me.
i can't stop staring at her
she doesn't know i exist.
i'm gonna pull myself away.

the dance

i want to be
Real
authentic
Truthful
it will not always
be pretty
or alluring
but honest.
Sharing our deepest desires
our greatest fears
regrets and insecurities
with no inhibitions.
Do i have to play
a game
of cat and mouse
a chase
to manipulate you
into wanting me?
submissively
surrender
stare at you intently
to cause excitement
and novelty?
i don't want to...be deceptive
I care more about you
than winning the prize.

the struggle

i am here
but I want to be
there.
you love her
Not me.
you want to talk
i don't want to listen.
you see someone
who doesn't exist.
I spoke my truth
you didn't understand
i am upset
for no reason.
I want you
but you want
someone else.

the ache

it came
out of nowhere
when i found out
you were leaving
i knew
it was coming
but it is almost
Here
and i can't bear it
its spreading
from my gut
to my heart
to the tips
of my fingers
Now I long for you
so thirsty
so hungry.
For me to look
you in the eyes
and know
that i won't see you
everyday
anymore
deflates me.
i miss you...
already.

vacancy

i miss you.
i long for you.
i want to hear your voice
say my name.
i want to see your face
in front of me.
i want to look at you.
i desire to touch you
to be close to you
and just Be.

letting go

i have this thing in my heart
that hurts
it didn't used to be that way
the thing in my heart
used to fill me with energy
and butterflies
i would feel in a daze
Drunk off the high
of feeling in love.
Now that thing
has changed
into a hunger
that can't be fed
It growls and yearns
for attention from that one
who leaves me starved.

I have to tear away that thing in my heart
and throw it far far away
so I can feel free
to love someone
who loves me back
Love from one side
Hurts so much
when the object of my affection
doesn't feel the same way.

So...

Let go! I scream
but my feelings
Cling to me
it's so hard to throw it away...
what if it doesn't come back
and his heart has changed?
Then it wasn't meant to be
I answer
and you deserve so much more
than what you
are being given.

Love

The purest element
It shines brighter
than anything
Its value
is infinite
Yet it costs nothing
Everyone yearns
for it
Yet it cannot
be taken
It is freely
Given
One cannot expect it
or force it
out of anyone.
You must start
with loving yourself
First
Surround yourself
with a circle of
Self-love
and do not
let anyone
Treat you differently.
I whisper to myself...
I will not respond to hate or affliction
but will embrace
Love.

unspoken words

every time I think of you
i want to reach out
but I stop myself
when I think about
my love not being
reciprocated.
Rejection
a piercing knife
into my soul
is a possibility
a risk
i can't fathom.
i'm afraid of...
My choice
the consequences
the conclusion.

the dilemma

the hardest thing
i've had to do
was let you go...
You must be free
to breathe
to discover
to choose your own path.
if you decide
to come to me
i will know your Love
Trust
Intention
without having
to ask.

The Warrior

You had a dream
You made it happen
Working harder
Smarter
Tougher
than anyone I know.
A risk taker
An extremist
Opinionated
some would say.
But I couldn't have asked
for a better example
to follow.
You battled them all
for the sake of principle.
You've never complained
Chuckled at pain
Would walk through fire
Endure any hardship
for us.
I admire and respect
Your courage
Your wisdom
Your frugality
The ultimate provider
I will never feel
Hopeless
Defenseless
Because of you.

My Hero

Generous
beyond anything
imaginable
i only hope to attain
a speck of wisdom
from the depths
of your soul.
A fortress of
Unconditional love
surrounds me from harm
Your sacrifice
and hard work
Built and shaped me
and instilled in me
A strength
i never knew i had.
Your undying support
makes me feel
Invincible
in the hardest of times.
i can't express my gratefulness
but can only become
the best version of myself
to show my appreciation
for YOU.

The Dream

your curly hair
your beautiful smile
as a child
your joy lit up the room.
I changed.
You changed.
and then
we became strangers.
I love you more
than anything.
I will always be here
Anytime you need me.
it has broken me
that we haven't spoken
in years
i only have memories
of you
i don't know
the adult you've become.
if I have wronged you
in the past
i am sorry.
i don't know why
we are here.
i don't know
what to say...
what to do...
to fix this.
But one day
I hope we can
bond together
and never let go.

Because we are all
we have.

My Angel

she's my best friend
through it all
so many heartaches
crying myself
to sleep at night
feeling hopeless
Alone
Misunderstood
Dizzy from trying
to make sense of it all
she laid by my side
showered me
with affection
couldn't say a word
but her love said it all.
it was all I needed...
an animal's intuition
to save me.

create or consume

in America
You have the power
to decide
will you choose
to Create
your own vision
your own path
to contribute
to the world
your uniqueness
or will you
sit back
and take
and complain
and be complacent
and let your existence
go to waste.

the grind

Wake up
Get through the day
Set goals
Make them happen
Come home
Zone out
Go to sleep
and repeat.

is life about
making a list
being organized
and checking things off?
Are we content
with the certainty
that this brings...
or is there another part
of ourselves
waiting to be discovered
and acknowledged?

detach

a moment is
Needed
Unplug
from all influence
Technology
Conformity
Pressure
Dependencies
Seek solitude
to discover
You
Not the idea
but the real
Individual
You are.
Take responsibility
to induce
the change you desire.
Be who you dream
of being
and
Become.

alone

How do we feel
when there is
no one around
Do we fidget
uncomfortable
looking to be
Entertained
or crave attention
from those around us.
Or do we feel
Free...
To breathe
To Exist
To relish
in the beauty of our
environment
To discover
Who we are
when no one
is looking at us
Judging us
Analyzing us.

simplicity

i want to just
Experience
Enjoy
each precious moment
Feel it
in its entirety
not distracted by
anything or
anyone.
nowhere to be
but right here
right now
and just let myself
Exist.

my love

Nature accepts me
where people do not.
Nature doesn't judge me
because I am different.
Nature frees me
from the confines of society
and how I'm told to be.
Nature surrounds me in Truth
there are no arguments
but reality and honesty.
I trust Nature.
it is loyal
and has Integrity.
Nature is love
and authentic love is pure.

the Wind

It can chill you
or make you feel
a part of something
Bigger
When you feel lonely
it can be a friendly companion
to remind you
that you are never
Alone.
It awakens our senses...
The cool electricity
flows through
every limb of my body
and makes me shiver.
i envy the wind...
It has no boundaries
or limits
or expectations.
It is completely free.

the Tree

We are each grounded
in the earth
by our identity
and uniqueness
as we stand tall
We should be proud
of our
Individual walks through life
and the choices
we have made.
Instead of rings
we have wrinkles
that we earned
through perseverance
and making mistakes
Like a Tree
we should adopt thick skin
and be rooted
by our values.
They silently
make a statement
without uttering a word.

leaf

when i look up
my eyes see You
in the tree
with all the others.
Most will see just a tree
with lots of leaves
but I see You
all on your own
with a gracefulness I admire
Never worried that the others
will stand out
around you
or mimic your actions.
i see your strength and beauty
as you exist in unison
with a peace of your own
in the serenity of your surroundings.

the hike

As i plant
one foot ahead
of the other
i slowly walk
Feeling the firmness
of the earth below
i am transported
out of my current
Reality
to one of
Beauty
of Truth
of Love.
i hear sweet sounds
from the birds
i hear the wind
call my name
i see vibrant colors
mesmerizing me...
the trees stand around me
like the protection of a friend
the undiscovered path revives me
from my corrupted soul
i hear...
the crunching of leaves
feel the crispness of the air
see the vividness of flowers...
the simplicity of nature
cleanses me
from the dirt
and pollution

of Society
and Technology.

Peace

i find true peace
in the stillness of my soul
In my refection
i see that although
i am flawed
i am perfect.
Just the way
i'm supposed to be
My outside appearance
Ages
Yet my inside self
grows more beautiful
day by day.
i feel truly proud
to be me.
i am awkward
but I like it.
Accept yourself fully
and you will find
Total freedom
to enjoy the person
whom you are never
without.
Yourself.

the path

There are many paths
but which will
you Choose
It doesn't matter
because you will be
redirected to another
if you listen
to your heart.
We are so afraid
of being wrong
or making a mistake
but mistakes
turn into depth
if you don't give up.
Your path is unique
Enjoy it.
Don't compare
Your experience
with others
but treasure the Journey
You have chosen.

the Awakening

I open my eyes
to the Serenity
of Being
Existing
Accepting
I no longer
Want more
have hunger
am thirsty
or feel that something
someone
is missing
from my life
I've been created
to be me
and no one else
I look inside myself
for the answers
that my Creator
has hidden
for me to discover
like a treasure hunt.
I love the
accumulation of Knowledge
I'm bestowed over time.
A present given to me
Daily
Forever.

Interaction
makes us stronger
as long as we
Hold on tightly
and never lose
our Identity.

The Discovery

As days pass by
Life is short
why waste time
trying to figure
everything out...
Just be yourself
Thoroughly.
Enjoy each moment
of everyday to come.
Do what makes you happy
No one else's opinion matters
it fades to the background.
Everything will settle down
and become what was meant to be.
Just let go...
See where life takes you
when you love yourself.

Butterfly

When it is created
it feels shy
it feels comfort
Hiding
burying itself
in its cocoon.
to others it seems
Strange
Awkward
in isolation
from the world.
Deeper within
it is discovering
Who it is
What it believes
How it feels
on its own
without the sway
from others.
It emerges
Confident
in its beliefs
its convictions
its values
and flies in
Total freedom
without a care
or thought
of what others think.

Acknowledgments

Thank you to my parents for all your support. I haven't been the easiest child, but through all my struggles I've learned that I'm really lucky to have you both as parents.

Thank you to a "nameless" person who introduced me to the concept of Mindfulness. I believe there are people you are meant to meet in life, even for a short moment in time, to learn and grow from and you are one of these people to me.

Most importantly, thank you to my Creator. Something/someone created me and I want to be a stronger/wiser/more loving person because of all the different ups downs, highs lows, happy sad moments I've experienced which have made me fully content to be myself.